PLANNING SOCIAL EVENTS

A Beginners Guide

DEBI BRAASCH

I.
WHAT ARE SOCIAL EVENTS?

Social events are any occasions where two or more people get together to celebrate, honor, or just socialize. Food and drink are usually included. Here is a short list of social events:

- Birthdays
- Weddings
- Church Suppers
- Housewarmings
- Holiday Parties
- Award Ceremonies
- Bon Voyage Parties
- Receptions
- Anniversaries
- Grand Openings
- Fourth of July

- Afternoon Tea
- Picnics

What to plan for when planning a social event?

- Location
- Guest list
- Invitations
- Menu
- Food preparation, serving, and clean up
- Entertainment
- Out of town guest housing and transportation

When planning a social event, it is helpful to have the following skills:

- Being Organized
- Working well within a timeline
- Having good communication skills
- Creativity
- Keeping your cool in emergencies
- Good Business skills (if doing events professionally)

2 .

GETTING STARTED

First answer the following questions:

- What, or who, is the event for?

  Holiday party at the office, or birthday party for mom?

- When is the event?

  You will need a date, and a starting and ending time.

- Where is the event?

  Is the party at your home or will you need to rent a location?

- How many guests are you inviting?

  Keep in mind your budget if you have one and the size of the event space.

- What is the style of the event?

  Is it a sit down banquet, a cocktail party, or a buffet?

- How much money do you have to spend on the total event or per person?

  Be conservative since your social event may have unforeseen costs.

- Where do you want most of the budget to go?

  Gourmet food? Great music? A special location? Celebrity entertainment? Door prizes?

- What kind of food?

  A potluck where guests share in bringing the food? Or you prepare the food, or hire a caterer?

- What kind of music?

  Book a band? A D.J.? Or just play CDs?

- How do you see the event happening?

  Daydream. See the event in your mind's eye. How would you like it to go?

- While planning your social event keep clear organized notes.

- Lastly, create a timeline. An example follows:

  Monday- Invite 10 guests for cake and ice cream on Saturday.

  Tuesday- Order cake from the bakery.

Wednesday- Buy plates etc. from party store.

Thursday- Confirm guest list by phone.

Friday- Buy ice cream and snacks.

Saturday- Pick up cake and vacuum house, guests arrives at 2:00pm.

How long should an event last? The average length of most events is about 4 hours. Your guest's energy and enthusiasm will wane after that. Cocktail parties however, which are often before dinner, can last between 1-2 hours. Cocktail parties in lieu of a formal dinner can be planned to go 4 hours.

3.

LOCATION, LOCATION, LOCATION

Locations for social events need to be planned well in advance. In addition to food and beverage, choosing a location is the most important consideration. If the party is being held at your home this step is done. However, some popular wedding venues need to be reserved a year in advance. You can never be too early with this step. Visit more than one location to see which one better fits your needs and budget.

When visiting an event location, keep in mind the number of guests you will be inviting and the style of party you will be having.

- Cocktail parties require at least 5 sq. ft. of space per person.
- Sit down dinners require 13-15 sq. ft. of space per person.

Also, most locations that are "rented out" have occupancy limits to the number of persons allowed in the room. Check with the management. Or the occupancy limit may be posted by the main entrance of the space.

After you have chosen a location for your event, it is necessary to visit the location a second time. Take pencil and paper with you and draw a floor plan of the space. You can also take photos. Make sure to include the following:

Inside

- Exits
- Entrances
- Windows
- Posts
- Fire exits
- Kitchen
- Bathrooms

Outside

- Pond
- Pool
- Fences
- Driveways
- Trees

- Shrubbery

Be as accurate as possible. You will need to use the plan and photos later when deciding where to place the beverage bars, stage, dance floor, buffet, and guest tables. Also note handicap access.

Plan for these possible complications:

- Dangers- pond, lake, pool, uneven ground for walking, lack of fire exits
- Is there enough space to park? (You may need a permit in some areas.)
- Unhappy neighbors with noise and traffic
- Local laws for noise, parking, and event location hours

A short list of some great locations:

- Convention Center
- Hotel
- Country club
- Rotunda of state capitol
- Museum
- Park
- Private home
- Back yard
- Church

- Private homes that are "rented out"
- Boat
- Office
- Movie theater
- Retail store
- Party room in mall
- Arcade center
- Historical site
- Gardens
- Closed off street
- Historic train
- Casino
- The beach
- A Renaissance Faire

4.

INVITATIONS

Whether you are sending out your invitations via e-mail, social media, or snail mail, you will need to include the following:

- Tell what the event is for or whom it is for.
- State the location of the event.
- What is the date of the event?
- Include the starting and ending time.
- Name any special persons or entertainment expected at the event.
- Indicate if it is a surprise party.
- Specify if guests are to bring anything, like a potluck dish, or wedding gifts.
- You may include a personal, handwritten note on each individual invitation expressing your sincere desire that they attend. For example: "The party won't be a success without you".

- Mention if special attire is required i.e. black or white tie, costumes, swimsuits, informal, business, or dressy casual.

- Ask for an RSVP at least 1 week in advance of the event. Contact all those who do not respond by that day. You must know one way or the other if they are attending. An accurate guest count is key to planning successful social events!

- Finally, if appropriate, be creative with the design of your invitations. Have them be a peek into the content or theme of the event to come.

Note: You can usually count on 10% of those you have invited to be unavailable due to other commitments or circumstances.

5.

THE DATE OF THE EVENT

- Some social events, like a wedding, will have a date picked by you without consideration as to your guests' schedules. Smaller events, such as a birthday party, may be scheduled with guests' availability in mind. Pick the most convenient date for most of your guests. You must plan far in advance for a social event during holiday time, December, and wedding months, June, and October. In some cases, it is necessary to reserve an event space a year in advance.

- When picking dates consider major events in your area that may compete with your event. For example, major sporting events, concerts, or festivals.

- Most invitations need to be sent out 1 month in advance of the event. You may also send a "save the date" card several months ahead of the invitation. That way your guests can put the date of the event on their calendar. This practice is popular with weddings.

- If guests must make travel plans, send invitations 6-8 weeks in advance of the event.

- Around holiday time, Thanksgiving through New Year's, you cannot send out the invitations too early. Six to eight weeks is good. Social calendars fill-up quickly at this time of the year.

- Note: In terms of the time of day of an event, consider if children and/or older folks will be attending. Mid-day or earlier evening start times are better for these age groups.

6.

PLANNING THE MENU
WHAT TO CONSIDER

- Does your location have power for grills or slow cookers?

- How many guests are you expecting? Any children?

- Is the guest list mostly men, women, or a mix?

- Plan a menu around the time of day, season, theme, and occasion. For example, you may want to have cooler, lighter foods in the summer, and warm soups and stews in the winter.

- Food that is fresh, local, and in season is a better choice than frozen prepackaged foods.

- Budget your money for the menu at a per person cost or for the entire event. For instance, $20.00 per person, or $2,000.00 total.

- Plan a menu with a variety of tastes, colors, shapes, textures, and themes. Sticking with a specific culture or theme makes food preparation easier, like Mexican, Italian, Chinese etc.

- Have foods that are "bullet proof". This means they can hold up for several hours without spoiling. As an example, fresh whipped cream will not hold its volume for more than a couple of hours at best.

- Choose recipes that you can do ahead of time and then reheat in the oven at the last minute. Or make foods that do well in a slow cooker.

- If the recipe requires cooking on site, make sure you have all the necessary equipment.

- Will the dish transport easily to the party site, or flop on the way? A good example of this is multi-tiered cakes. It is better to assemble some foods like this at the party site.

- Choose recipes with ingredients that are easy to get and fit into your budget.

- Dishes with meat and ice cream will need to be refrigerated or kept on ice.

Note: Ice cream must be packed in dry ice to stay frozen. The exception to this is homemade ice cream that is kept in the ice cream maker and packed with ice and salt.

If you decide to hire a caterer, your main concern will be what food you want served at the event, and not so much logistics. The caterer will handle that.

On the opposite end, you may choose to have a "potluck". This is an event where the guests bring part of the menu.

- Have guests bring one or two dishes of any type of food.

- You may consider having guests bring a side dish and/or dessert, and you are responsible for the main dish.

- Use a signup sheet with specific dishes or categories of food listed for guests to bring.

7.

EQUIPMENT AT LOCATIONS OTHER THAN YOUR HOME

- It is important to gather all the equipment that you will need in advance.

- Make a list of what you will need and check the items off as you put them in a box, or in your car.

- Check with the staff at your location. See if you can deliver your equipment to the party site ahead of time.

- Even if the event is at your home, gather your equipment ahead and set everything aside in a convenient place.

- Always know the nearest grocery store to the event site just in case you forget something. Even the best event planner can forget equipment, especially small but essential items like serving spoons.

- Planning and doing ahead is important for a successful event. You will be less stressed, able to handle last minute details and changes by being organized and having a plan.

In most cases "equipment" will refer to kitchen and serving items. Your equipment needs are primarily based on your menu. You will need to refer to your menu to make the list. Breads require baskets, butter may need to be put on ice, and hot foods may need chaffing dishes etc. Remember to pack cleaning supplies, containers, and food wraps for leftovers.

For all special events, call your vendors and people whom you have hired at least one week ahead to confirm their delivery of goods or services. This will mean the caterer, rental company, valets, booked entertainment, service personnel, and kitchen staff. If you are renting a location, it is always good to contact the management to confirm the time you will be arriving at the site.

8.

ESTIMATED FOOD AND BEVERAGE AMOUNTS

Non-Alcoholic beverages:

- In general, drinks- 8 oz per person per hour of event.

- Soda or bottled water- 1 bottle per person per hour of event.

- Coffee- 2 cups per person per event.

Alcoholic Beverages:

- 1 bottle of wine or champagne per two guests per two hours.

- 1 cocktail per person per hour.

- 1 bottle of beer per person per hour

Things to keep in mind with alcoholic beverages:

- How long is the event?
- Are the guests heavy or light drinkers?
- Is it a cocktail party with alcoholic beverages as the focus?
- Do you want to offer just beer and wine, or a full bar?
- To make your budget stretch what about serving alcoholic punch?

It is certainly better to have more beverages on hand than needed. Plan about 25% more than you think you will need. Some beverage distributors will allow you to return unopened bottles. Remember the bar equipment, ice, olives, lemon, and limes!

Salads:

- With a meal 3-4 oz. per person.
- As an appetizer 3 oz. per person.

Dressing:

- ¼ cup per person.

Appetizer:

- 4 oz. per person.

Bread and Rolls:

- 1 ½ pieces per person.

Sorbet and ice cream:

- 2 oz. per person.

Soup:

- With a meal 6 oz. per person.
- As a main course 12-16 oz. per person.

Pasta:

- With a meal 2 oz. per person.
- As a main course 4-6 oz. per person.

Meat and Fish:

- Lunch 4 oz. per person.
- Dinner 6 oz. per person, 8-10 oz. for men.

Chicken:

- Women 1 breast or thigh per person.
- Men 1 ½-2 breasts or thighs per person.

Vegetables and Potatoes:

- 2-4 oz. per person depending on the rest of the menu.

Desserts:

- 4 oz. or 1 ½ servings per person.

Hors d'oeuvres:

- With dinner 6-8 pieces per person.
- Cocktail party 10 plus pieces per person.

Children:

- Sandwiches ½-2 per child depending on age.
- Salads 2-4 oz.
- Desserts 2-4 oz.
- Drinks, main dishes, and vegetables are the same as for women.

What to keep in mind when planning a menu?

- Choose foods that are "bullet proof" and will hold up for several hours.
- Men eat more than women and prefer "heavier" foods.
- Women may favor "lighter" foods such as salads.
- Always have kid friendly food if children are invited.

Special diets to consider:

- Vegetarian

- Vegan
- Halal
- Kosher
- Non-dairy
- Grain free
- Gluten free
- Sugar free

9.
ENTERTAINMENT

Types of Entertainment for Social Events may include:

- Murder Mystery
- Comedian
- Magician
- Mini Golf
- Celebrity Look-A-Like
- Jazz Pianist
- Orchestra Ensemble
- Board Games
- Variety Show
- Souvenir Photos
- Caricature Artist
- Carnival Rides and Games
- Swimming
- Face Painting

- Poetry Reading
- D.J.
- Vocalist
- Movie
- Mime Performer
- Pony Rides
- Clown
- Athletic Games
- Skating
- Dress up Characters
- Stage Show
- Live Band
- Dancers
- Las Vegas Casino
- Puppet Show
- Petting Zoo

Make the arrangements for the entertainment yourself or hire a professional. Booking and talent agencies are good sources. This may seem obvious, but make sure the entertainment you hire is appropriate for the occasion.

10.

OUT OF TOWN GUESTS

- In your invitations, give the names of local hotels that have special rates for your event.

- Include directions to and the address of, the party location.

- If possible, have a wedding and reception in the same location. Or hire vans, small limos, or luxury coaches as a shuttle. This works well if there are many guests from out of town.

- For a reunion or conference book a hospitality room in the hotel or convention center. A hospitality room is a small space set-up with food and beverages for your guests to socialize between events.

- If you can, have something special in the hotel room for your guests. For instance, a basket of fruit, candy, coupons to nearby restaurants, or tickets to shows and attractions.

- Have your VIP guests picked up at the airport.

- If guests are staying at your home, all the above is still appropriate.

II.

RENTALS AND TABLES

What can you rent? Turns out, almost anything. Here is a partial list:

- Tables and chairs
- All dinnerware
- Table linen
- Food machines
- Floral arrangements
- Balloons
- Classic Cars
- Entertainers
- Props for theme parties
- Outdoor heaters
- Tents of all sizes

- Screens
- Costumes
- Security
- Photo booths
- Trash cans

When choosing a rental company get a referral from friends, catering companies, or online reviews.

Banquet and buffet tables come in both rectangular and round. Most rental companies carry 4, 6, 8, and 10-foot rectangular tables. Round tables are typically measured in 36, 60, and 72 inches. 4-foot tables are most often used behind a bar for extra storage space and are called a back bar. Some rental companies also have serpentine or heart shaped tables for rent. With these tables you can get more creative with your buffet set-up. Rental companies can also supply you with table linens in a large variety of colors, styles, sizes, and patterns.

- For a "walk around" cocktail party, have enough seating for ½ of the guests, unless you are expecting seniors, or other individuals with limited mobility. In this case you will need seating for everyone.

- As for a sit-down dinner the best choice is round tables. They are elegant and allow your guests to socialize more easily. However, if you are pressed for space, you may have to use rectangular banquet tables which take up less area in the room.

- For buffet tables, use both round and banquet tables for displaying the food and serving. If available, you can also use serpentine tables to add some interest.

- Usually, you will need table center pieces. This could include- low flower arrangements, potted plants, mirror with candles, artwork, party theme displays, food platters such as anti-pasta, veggies, chips and dip, or fruit.

- Center pieces at the tables are where you can be creative. They should reflect the theme of the event or be very elegant. Keep center pieces low so that guests on opposite sides of the table can see and talk to one another. Or have the center pieces on high thin pedestals above the line of sight of your guests. Remember that the designs of center pieces and event decorations go in and out of style like all modes of design.

12.

HIRING SERVICE PERSONNEL

Service personnel include waiters, kitchen staff, chefs, and bartenders. It is best to go with a reputable service personnel company when looking for event staff. Check online or call a caterer for advice. Most often caterers hire and maintain their own event staff. So, they can arrange for event staff for your event. Most of the time caterers will require that you use their chefs who are familiar with serving the food they are providing.

Guidelines for hiring your own event staff:

- Hire dependable, hardworking, friendly, and experienced staff.
- Check their references.
- Asking dependable friends and family to help serve is fine.

- Have all service staff wear the same uniform so guests will know who is serving the party. Some options could include "Black and Whites" (tuxedoes), matching polo shirts, costumes, or T-shirts with the name of the event printed on them.

- For valet parking, go with a reputable valet company or ask the caterer you are using. If hiring valets, yourself, have 2 valets for every 50 cars and one to open the doors.

Guidelines for how many staff you will need:

- For a cocktail party you will need 1 server for every 50 guests.

- Sit down dinners require 1 server for every 16-20 guests. Since most round banquet tables seat 8-10 guests, one experienced server can handle 2 tables.

- In general, you will need 1 bartender for every 100 guests. Two bartenders can manage one bar. But if you have over 200 guests it is advisable to have two bars in different parts of the event space.

- You will need 1 chef for every 100 guests at a cocktail party.

- For a sit-down dinner, you will need 1 chef for every 100 guests.

13.

SETTING UP

Guidelines for placing tables:

- Place all tables away from entry doors, fire exits, and when possible, kitchen and bathroom doors.

- Have at least 4 ft between dining tables. Guests need room to push back their chairs to get up from the table. 18 inches is the bare minimum for this "push back space".

- You must have at least 24 inches between place settings. Most round 72-inch banquet tables will seat 8-10 guests.

- In a large room, do not place dining tables too far apart. Tables closer together give a feeling of coziness. However, cocktail tables can be scattered around the room in small groups. If having a dance floor, leave enough room for guests to enter and exit.

- Place buffet tables near the kitchen.

- For Hors d' Oeuvres use round tables that can be placed in the middle of the room so both sides can be accessed. However, banquet tables alongside a wall are fine as well.

- You may also consider placing Hors d' Oeuvres tables around the room to get guests moving from one part of the room to the next.

- Place bars with enough area for a cue line to form.

- You will need 1 bar for every 150-200 guests. You can rent a bar, or simply use a buffet table.

- Have 1 buffet line for every 50 guests.

Note: If the food is being served by wait staff, you can only have one serving line per buffet table, or 50 guests per side. This does cut down on food waste as guests often take more than they can eat. But you may decide to have guests serve themselves. Having two lines, one on each side of the table, cuts down on long wait times. In this case you would calculate 100 guests per buffet table. Remember to provide two serving utensils per dish if choosing to have a line on each side of the table.

Guidelines for setting buffet tables:

- 2 dinner plates per person.

- 1 dessert plate per person.

- 1 each of spoons, forks, and knives per person. Add extras for salad and dessert.

- 2-3 glasses per person. Place glassware at a bar or "help yourself" table.

- Place food and tableware in a commonsense order on buffet tables. For example: plates, entrée, side dishes, salads, condiments, breads, butters, silverware, napkins.

- Drinks can come at the end of the buffet or on separate tables.

Guidelines for setting cocktail party tables:

- 2-3 plates per person.

- Silverware if food being served is not finger food.

- Cocktail napkins

- 4 glasses per person, or 1 for every hour of the event.

Guidelines for a sit-down dinner:

- Plates, silverware, etc. will depend on the menu.

- It may help to consult an etiquette book for detailed information on dinnerware and place settings.

14.

THE DAY OF THE EVENT

If the event is not at your home, double check that you have everything you need in your vehicle.

Food and serving pieces

- Linens and tableware, unless delivered to the site
- Decorations
- Directions to the event site for everyone setting up
- Party clothes to change into if necessary
- Check book or bank card in case you need to pay a vendor
- Contact numbers for all vendors, service staff, and event location

Make sure you leave plenty of time to get to your location and plenty of time for set up. With major events, drive to the event location and clock how long it takes you. Allow for rush hour traffic. Most events will need 2 hours for set up. With major events, allow 1 or more days. If you can, set up the event the day before. Then you can have the tables in place and dressed in linen, tableware, and center pieces. Buffets can be set up with chaffing dishes, serving pieces, and any decorations. Bars can be set up with equipment and beverages. With everything ready the day before, all you will need to do is place the food on the buffet and ice down the drinks.

Have the event set up ½ hour before starting time. That way you can relax and greet your guests who may come early. It is also a good idea to set up the party in casual clothes and change into party clothes right before the guests arrive.

At most events there are two main areas. The front of the house is where you will be setting up tables, chairs, linens, decorations, center pieces, florals, bars, busing stations, and trach cans. And back of the house which serves as a kitchen and storage of extra items. This can be anyplace from a full kitchen to a hallway or closet setup. It is used to keep extra food hot or cold, to plate food and to store all extra items related to the event.

15.

AFTER THE EVENT

Simple rule: Leave everything the way you found it or better.

And remember to take everything you brought with you and thank the management of the location.

FINAL NOTE: If you are having disposable cutlery and plates you need to have adequate trash cans and busing trays on stands around the space. Even if you have a sit-down dinner with wait staff serving the tables, you will still want several busing trays around the room. The number of trash cans or busing trays you need is not a hard and fast rule. It can be different depending on the size of the location, number of people, and other factors. Use your best judgement to decide how many you may need.

ABOUT THE AUTHOR

Debi Braasch's professtional career in Event Planning began in 1986 with Glenda's of Course Catering and Events in Los Angles, CA. Later she was the assistant director of the Berkeley Conference Center, Berkely, CA.

Debi now resides with her husband in Harrisburg, PA.